The Bible

Text
Sr. Karen Cavanagh, CSJ

Cover Illustration
William Luberoff

Text Illustrations
Edward Letwenko

Regina Press

New York

The Bible is the book which tells the story of God's great love for all people since the very beginning of time. People all over the world read the Bible.

Those who wrote the many stories of the Bible were inspired by God and wrote about God's care. That is why the Bible is called the "Word of God."

The Old Testament is the first part of the Bible. It tells how God worked in the world before the coming of Jesus.

Every day the Bible is read in churches all over the world. Each Sunday we hear God's word and remember God's great love.

In the first book of the Bible we are told of God's creation of the world. God gave us heaven and earth; the water and the light.

God created plants and trees and animals to live on the earth. God saw that it was very good.

". . . YOU, GOD, HAVE

God made Adam and Eve to care for and be over all the works of creation. We call Adam and Eve our first parents.

After the great flood God sent Noah and his family a sign of love and promise — a beautiful rainbow.

". . . . MAY YOUR FAITHFUL LOVE BE ON US,

God promised Abraham and Sarah that their children would number more than the stars in the night sky. Abraham is our father in the faith.

Jacob loved his son, Joseph, and made him a coat of many colors. His jealous brothers sold him as a slave to the Egyptians.

Moses parted the waters and led his people toward the promised land. On Mt. Sinai God gave him the law. The love of God is the law.

Ruth told her mother-in-law, Naomi, "Your people will be my people. Your God will be my God." Her son was to become King David's grandfather.

"... MY SONG IS ABOUT FAITHFULNESS,

David was God's choice to be the King of Israel. It is taught that David wrote and sang the psalms to God.

God protected the Jewish people from the defeat of their powerful enemy. Judith told them to rely upon the strength of God. God's strength helped her to kill the enemy leader.

". . .I WILL MEDITATE ON YOUR LAW AND THINK OF

Whenever we read or hear the word of God
and in my heart."

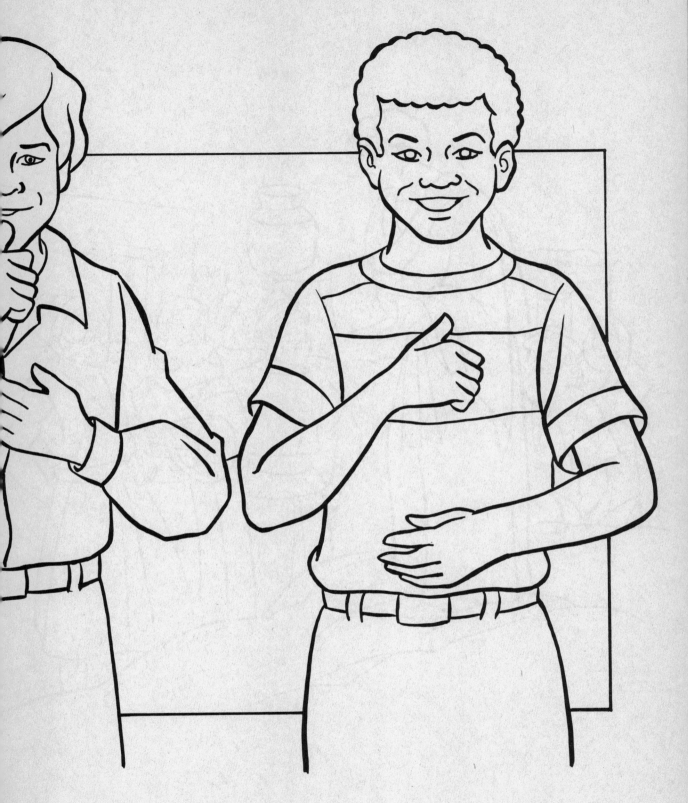

ray, "May the Lord be in my mind, on my lips

"...BEFORE A WORD IS EVEN

Jeremiah was afraid to speak for God because he was so young. God told him not to fear. God put the words in Jeremiah's mouth. He became God's prophet.

Isaiah was one of the most famous prophets. He foretold that God would send a savior. This savior was to be Jesus.

The New Testament is the second half of the Bible. In it we read of Jesus' life and message of love and peace.

When Mary was a young girl she studied God's word at the temple school. Her life and her love would help to fulfill God's promise.

"...TEACH ME YOUR WAY, GOD,

The Gospel of Luke tells us how the young Jesus stayed behind in the temple to listen to the priests and talk about God's word.

Jesus proclaimed God's word in the temple at Nazareth. He did this as he began His work of teaching and preaching God's love.

In Matthew's gospel we see Jesus performing miracles and curing people as he lives God's word of concern and love.

". . . THE SEED IS GOD'S WORD"

Jesus taught His friends with stories called parables. These stories have a message about how God works in our lives.

In Mark's gospel Jesus tells that many would deny God's word and promise in His message. He knew He would suffer and die for God's ways.

When Jesus rose from the dead He appeared to Mary Magdalen. She ran to tell the good news to the other apostles and friends of Jesus. Jesus fulfilled God's promise.

John tells us in his gospel that Jesus is *The Word* of God who became human for us and lived among us. John the Baptist was his witness.

John said that if all the things which Jesus did were written down the world itself would not hold all the books. God's word is great.

The Acts of the Apostles tells of the early Christian community sharing all things and God's word with each other. They became the new teachers of God's word.

As the communities grew God's love and message were
written down in letters to the community. These
letters in the Bible are called the epistles. Many were
written by Paul.

Draw and color your favorite scene from the Bible:

Write your own story:

_____

_____

_____

_____

_____